MRS KLEIN

NICHOLAS WRIGHT

Nicholas Wright was born in Cape Town and trained as an actor in London. He joined the Royal Court Theatre as Casting Director, and subsequently became the first director of the Theatre Upstairs, which he ran over a period of five years. In 1975-77 he was Joint Artistic Director of the Royal Court, with Robert Kidd. His first full-length play, *Treetops*, was produced at Riverside Studios in 1978. *The Gorky Brigade* was presented at the Royal Court in 1979, and *One Fine Day* at Riverside the following year. In 1981-82 he travelled and lived for a year in Zimbabwe, where he wrote *The Custom of the Country* – a romantic comedy on colonial themes which was produced by the RSC in 1983. His version of Balzac's 'Splendeurs and Misères des Courtisanes' was presented by Joint Stock in the same year, under the title *The Crimes of Vautrin*. *The Desert Air* – a comedy about covert activity during World War II – was produced by the RSC in 1984. Translations and adaptations include two plays by Marivaux (*Slave Island* and *The Double Inconstancy*) and Pirandello's *Six Characters in Search of an Author*, which was presented in 1987 at the National Theatre, where he is currently Literary Manager.

by the same author

The Custom of the Country
The Desert Air

NICHOLAS WRIGHT

MRS KLEIN

NICK HERN BOOKS

A division of Walker Books Limited

A Nick Hern Book

Mrs. Klein first published in 1988 as an original paperback by
Nick Hern Books, a division of Walker Books Limited,
87 Vauxhall Walk, London SE11 5HJ

Mrs. Klein copyright © 1988 by Nicholas Wright
Front cover illustration:
detail from *Girl with a white dog* by Lucian Freud
reproduced by courtesy of the Trustees of the Tate Gallery

Set in ITC New Baskerville and printed in Great Britain by
Expression Printers Limited, London N7 9DP

British Library Cataloguing in Publication Data
Wright, Nicholas, 1940–
    Mrs Klein.
    I Title
    822'.914
ISBN 1-85459-000-6

Mrs. Klein was first staged in the Cottesloe auditorium of the National Theatre of Great Britain.

First preview was 5 August 1988; press night was 10 August 1988.

The cast was as follows:

MRS. KLEIN	Gillian Barge
PAULA	Zoë Wanamaker
MELITTA	Francesca Annis

Directed by Peter Gill
Set designed by John Gunter
Costumes by Stephen Brimson-Lewis
Music by Terry Davies

Mrs. Klein is 52. Paula and Melitta are in their early thirties.
Place: London
Time: Spring 1934

This text went to press before the opening night, and may therefore differ slightly from the text as performed.

Nicholas Wright gratefully acknowledges the use of Phyllis Grosskurth's biography *Melanie Klein*, published by Hodder and Stoughton, 1985.

ACT ONE

MRS. KLEIN *is sorting through old papers.* PAULA *is listening.*

MRS. KLEIN. It's quite incredible what one keeps.

Tears up a photograph. Finds a piece of paper.

This is a poem he wrote.

Reads it.

Excuse me.

She cries. Holds her hand out. PAULA *takes it. She slowly stops crying.*

I think that's it till next time. So: our coffee should be ready. You'll have some?

PAULA. Thank you.

MRS. KLEIN. Now what's this?

PAULA. I've brought you something.

It's a cakebox.

MRS. KLEIN. But my dear you shouldn't have spent your money. No don't tell me.

Opens it.

Paula, this is fantastic of you. Poppy-seed cake, no reason you should believe this, was my mother's speciality.

Gives PAULA *the poem.*

You can read this.

She goes out. PAULA *reads.* MRS. KLEIN *comes back with coffee. Pours.*

MRS. KLEIN. I'm in a very adequate state, all things considered. I cough a lot but then I'm smoking more. I sleep enough, not much. I have my knock-out drops if I should need them but I'm holding off so far. No dreams, which is unusual for me. Normally I'm an active, colourful dreamer. Now each night the show is cancelled. Most annoying. Mi'k?

PAULA. No thank you.

MRS. KLEIN. Then I'll need another cup.

PAULA. It doesn't matter.

MRS. KLEIN. Sure?

PAULA. Quite sure.

MRS. KLEIN *gives her the cup.*

MRS. KLEIN. You're welcome. Chiefly what I feel is numbness. Here inside. As though some vital part of me had been removed. The tears don't help. All they do is make a thorough nuisance of themselves. And then they stop and leave me feeling exactly as I did before. Remote. Closed up. And dead. You'll have some cake?

PAULA. Yes thank you.

MRS. KLEIN. So: my work goes on. I read, I write, I entertain a few old friends, I see my patients. Clear a space. I'm on my own today. My cleaning woman has a family crisis in Southend. Or so she says. The truth is that she needs a break from my unnatural calm. And so do I. But there we are, I may not like it but I'm stuck with it. I don't know why. I don't have insight into my emotions, not just now. Some other time. So: eat.

They do.

But why no dreams? No, that's enough about me. The poem, you read it?

PAULA. Yes.

MRS. KLEIN. So tell me.

PAULA. It was written when he was young – .

MRS. KLEIN. He was. He was a boy, he was fifteen.

PAULA. It's a love-poem. Though the woman seems older than him. Who was she?

MRS. KLEIN. I doubt she ever existed. Not in life. Though to my son, of course, she breathed, she moved, she comforted. She was *the mother.*

PAULA. Yes I see.

MRS. KLEIN. She was myself. I would like you to do some work for me .

PAULA. What kind of work?

MRS. KLEIN. You're not too busy?

PAULA. No.

MRS. KLEIN. Thank God, thank God. Have some more cake.

PAULA. No thank you.

MRS. KLEIN has some more.

MRS. KLEIN. I'm famished. I've been eating scraps. Cheese on toast, sardines on toast, ridiculous. And so this morning up I got and cooked myself a hearty British breakfast. Then I looked at it. And then I gave it to the pekinese. He's not here now. He'll be living the life of Riley for the next ten days, in kennels, up by Primrose Hill. He won't be bothering you. His name is Nanki-Poo. A wandering minstrel he. You know your Gilbert and Sullivan?

PAULA. When you say he won't be bothering me – ?

MRS. KLEIN. Quite so. Let me explain.

A set of keys.

These are my spare keys to the front door. My cleaning woman has her own. Keys to the rooms upstairs, my bedroom, my consulting-room, I'm putting somewhere safe, she'll tell you if you ask, but for emergencies. She says she'll water the plants. If you could watch the window-boxes. Let me see.

Her notebook.

I made a list. I felt compelled to. And this in itself is strange, because my memory's good. I woke at four o'clock this morning, wondering, 'What am I making lists for, is there perhaps some paranoiac aspect to it?', but I couldn't think it through at that hour. I've stopped the milk. I've stopped the Times, I've stopped the Daily Mail. The central heating has instructions pinned above it. Sunny is with my daughter. Sunny is the car, the Sunbeam. Make of it what you will. Food is in the fridge, and when you leave at night please check the windows and of course the door. Now is there anything else domestic? Good.

PAULA. I'm sorry – . Do you want – ?

MRS. KLEIN. If I could do my list? And questions after.

At the desk.

Letters here. Periodicals here. Messages on this pad.

Letters.

These I would appreciate your posting for me.

A pin-box.

I've left some money here for odd expenses and your travel. I won't feel happy otherwise. I'll worry that you're feeling in some way imposed upon. So spend it freely. Here. Five shillings. Good, that's settled.

Another letter.

This I don't know what to do with. It arrived this morning. Marked: 'To await return'. It comes from Dr. Schmideberg. I don't like it. I don't even like the envelope. It looks as though it's about to burst with hostile matter. This is what professional enemies are like. They're vampires. They're dependent. They want love. And so they nag and pester. Should I read it? Should I leave it? Should I burn it? If I burn it, can I blame the post? I'll –. No I can't decide.

She puts it down.

At such a time I don't deserve to be so persecuted. Next. The proofs.

PAULA. The proofs?

MRS. KLEIN. You know the system?

PAULA. If you tell me what it is you want I'll –.

MRS. KLEIN. Fine, come look.

Proofs on the desk.

You've read the book?

PAULA. Of course, I –.

MRS. KLEIN. I thought so. This will be the second German-language edition.

A book.

This is the first. There are some misprints which I've put a ring round. So you must check both. I've marked in pencil where I want revisions.

Notes.

These are they. This arrow goes back, then skip, then on, yes?

Another book.

Some revisions, though not all, are in the second English edition, here.

A dictionary.

English-German, German-English.

Manuscript.

Here's the new chapter. So you must watch the numbering.

Another manuscript.

This is the foreword. Do you type?

PAULA. Two fingers.

MRS. KLEIN. Likewise. Three copies. Carbon here. You understand?

PAULA. Yes.

MRS. KLEIN. Sure?

PAULA. Quite sure. When is the copy-date?

MRS. KLEIN. Forget the copy-date, it's weeks ago, I want them posted to Vienna first post Wednesday at the latest.

PAULA. Fine. I'll show you what I've done on Tuesday.

MRS. KLEIN. I won't be here.

PAULA. You won't – ?

MRS. KLEIN. I have a funeral to attend.

PAULA. I'm sorry, yes, I see, so will you –

MRS. KLEIN. I shall be back the following weekend.

PAULA. Then you won't have seen them.

MRS. KLEIN. Plainly not.

PAULA. So if there's anything I get wrong – .

MRS. KLEIN. They'll print it wrong and I'll look stupid. But I'm not expecting that to happen.

PAULA. Why?

MRS. KLEIN. Because I trust you.

PAULA. But we've never met.

MRS. KLEIN. I've seen you at the Institute, you're highly thought of.
Will you do it?

PAULA. Yes.

MRS. KLEIN. You're a good girl. I didn't ask you if you'd like a glass
of sherry.

PAULA. No.

MRS. KLEIN. Too early? Likewise.

Pause.

You like my flowers? I shan't be looking at them, take some home.

PAULA. I haven't room.

MRS. KLEIN (*dry*). No room for a bunch of flowers? You're not by
any chance exaggerating?

PAULA. Perhaps a little.

MRS. KLEIN. Just a little.

Pause. Relaxed. They are both accustomed to long pauses.

Besides I liked your comments after Edward Glover read his paper
on suggestion. At that Scientific Meeting. You were very acute. You
shut him up for weeks, that's no mean tribute. When was it now? At
Christmas. Yes, the seminar-room was full of shopping-bags. That
was you?

PAULA. It was.

MRS. KLEIN. I knew it. Tell me, who is worse in your professional
estimation, Glover or Schmideberg? No I mustn't compromise
you. Glover's not a dunce exactly but he's too dogmatic. Like some
mid-Victorian, mutton-chop-whiskered tyrant of the breakfast
table, ghastly.

Laughs, then stops.

Dr. Schmideberg needs help.

Pause.

The heck with it.

She goes to the drinks cabinet and pours two sherries.

So we've never met? I felt I knew you.

PAULA. We've been introduced. But never –.

MRS. KLEIN. Never sat and talked. It's very pleasant. And I'm glad you arrived a fraction late. I was with a patient. Nine years old last week. So, not my youngest but my most demanding. He wouldn't stay in the consulting-room today, he felt it pressing in on him, he took against it. So we came down here. There, that's his train, his Daddy-train he calls it. He played, I played. If you'd been on time I wouldn't have let you in. Because my patients cannot be disturbed. The world must wait. I'm sure you feel the same. Now this is a Manzanilla which I'm rather proud of.

They sit and drink their sherry. Pause.

MRS. KLEIN. You have family back at home?

PAULA. I do.

MRS. KLEIN. You hear from them?

PAULA. My mother writes. My brothers .

MRS. KLEIN. Have you sisters?

PAULA. No.

MRS. KLEIN. That's not a simple 'no'.

PAULA. I had an older sister.

MRS. KLEIN. Were you close in age?

PAULA. She died before I was born.

MRS. KLEIN. So you're important to your mother.

PAULA. Yes.

MRS. KLEIN. To comfort her. Or so you see it. And you're married?

PAULA. Yes.

MRS. KLEIN. He's not an analyst?

PAULA. He's a doctor.

MRS. KLEIN. That isn't what I asked.

PAULA. He's not an analyst.

MRS. KLEIN. He doesn't approve?

PAULA. He doesn't approve.

MRS. KLEIN. And where've you put him?

PAULA. Where – ?

MRS. KLEIN. He's not in England?

PAULA. No. In Zurich.

MRS. KLEIN. Ah. So did he – ?

PAULA. He left Germany first. Because he had to. I stayed on. Because there wasn't so much pressure on me.

MRS. KLEIN. Though I heard you'd been arrested.

PAULA. It wasn't serious. Just a small misunderstanding. They searched the house and took some books and dropped the charge.

Pause.

MRS. KLEIN. It frightened you.

PAULA. Yes.

MRS. KLEIN. You're Jewish.

PAULA. Yes. But it was worse for him. My husband. He was more political than I am.

MRS. KLEIN. When you say your husband was political, do you mean he isn't now or that he's no longer your husband?

PAULA. We're divorced.

MRS. KLEIN. And how do you find it?

PAULA. Lonely.

MRS. KLEIN. Likewise.

Gives PAULA *her glass, marks a place on it with her finger.*

MRS. KLEIN. I can manage that much more. And help yourself.

PAULA *pours sherry.*

MRS. KLEIN. My son was fond of politics when he was younger. And his friends. Just like in any other intellectual family. But I've never been political myself. Although I've had good cause to. I've been spat at in the street. My children too. And now I hear each week from friends at home, the windows smashed, the star of Judah painted on the doors, the papers scattered, the maid hysterical, the children in tears. I know about it, thank you, and it won't get better. I can't stop it. You can't. Can your husband? In these terrible times we live in? And it doesn't interest me to try. That's not my style.

She sees her sherry, drinks.

Somebody said you had a daughter.

PAULA. What?

MRS. KLEIN. Your daughter.

PAULA. I'm sorry I didn't hear you. I've a daughter, yes. She's nine. She's in Berlin. She's with some Catholic friends.

MRS. KLEIN. And will she join you?

PAULA. Soon. Except –.

MRS. KLEIN. So what is your problem?

PAULA. I'll need a decent place to live.

MRS. KLEIN. Where are you now?

PAULA. In Bethnal Green.

MRS. KLEIN. I've never been there, what's it like?

PAULA. It's horrible. It's a slum.

MRS. KLEIN. And do you practise there?

PAULA. I try to.

MRS. KLEIN. It must be hard.

PAULA. It's impossible. Either my patients can't afford to pay me or they leave.

MRS. KLEIN. It's early days.

PAULA. I'm thirty-four. I don't have a proper coat. I've never lived like this.

MRS. KLEIN. You're angry.

PAULA. Yes.

MRS. KLEIN. You should apply to change your visa.

PAULA. I have.

MRS. KLEIN. Then you must ask again. I'll put a word in for you. No, don't thank me. I do little enough for you these days. Pass me that box.

It's the box with Hans's letters in it.

I feel that Hans would like his poem to go to you.

She gives PAULA *the scrap of paper.*

PAULA. I can't accept it.

MRS. KLEIN. No strings. It's his.

PAULA. Thank you.

She takes it.

MRS. KLEIN. But there's something on your mind.

PAULA. I don't know why you're doing this. Why you're letting me help you. Isn't there someone else who – ?

MRS. KLEIN. Who?

PAULA. You have your English friends.

MRS. KLEIN. I was holidaying in St. Ives last week and a very good English friend came with me. Mrs. Riviere. I like her, she's a loyal colleague and an adequate clinician, not outstanding. We stayed a week, then motored back and stopped in Salisbury. A bed and breakfast place, no heating, didn't like dogs and Mrs. Riviere discovered that she'd left her fox-fur back in Cornwall. This is a woman who takes a fox-fur on a walking holiday. So she rang the hotel, and suddenly it's the manager's wife. 'Is that Mrs. Klein?' 'No, it's her friend, I think I left my fox-fur on the terrace – '. But it's me the woman wants to talk to. There's been a telephone-call for me, from Budapest, a foreign lady, Mrs. Vago. 'Yes', I say, 'My sister-in-law. And what was so important that she telephones?' I'd left the number here, so – . 'Is it bad news?' I ask. The woman says: 'It is my duty – '. She was trying to be considerate. I say, don't go around the houses, I'm a grown-up woman, I'm sitting down. She says, it's about my son. He's had a climbing accident. I'm sitting in the hallway looking at a green baize board with postcards on it. Stonehenge. I was looking at it, thinking, 'What does *that* mean?' She was talking. 'Are you there?' She thought I'd fainted. I said: 'Tell me please: this accident my son had: was it fatal?' She replied: 'I'm sorry, Mrs. Klein, you won't believe this but I can't remember.' I said, 'Don't worry, I believe you, but I can't explain it to you, not right now, just tell me: have you written it down?' She says: 'I'll find it'. I waited. In a state of some suspense. I heard her shuffling papers, banging drawers. Then it struck me: how, without appearing callous, would I raise the subject of my friend's fox-fur? And I was worried about her fur because I didn't *really, absolutely* think she'd sympathise. Although she did. And she was admirable. But yet I didn't trust her. Why? Because I don't trust any of them. Not with this. Not now. They don't feel homelike. I want my home around me. I want the good things close and safe. I want to hear the German language. You speak German and you bring me poppy-seed cake. Also I like you.

She passes the box to PAULA.

MRS. KLEIN. Put it beneath the stairs and bring my coat and hat. And my umbrella. And my bags, no, leave them there but count them, there are two and a hatbox.

PAULA. Are you leaving now?

MRS. KLEIN. Yes now, the taxi's due in – . Check the gloves are in the pockets.

PAULA *gets her coat, etc. while* MRS. KLEIN *writes down a telephone number.* PAULA *comes back with coat, etc.*

MRS. KLEIN. You can reach me at this number. Budapest is not that far, my sister in-law speaks perfect German. As you see I wish to reassure you that I haven't died. Now do I need to spend a penny. No.

She dresses.

I won't suggest you see me to the station. You'd be better advised to start the work at once.

Checks in her notebook.

Scissors. Needles. Who needs needles.

Doorbell rings.

Ticket. Passport. Money. Glasses.

Doorbell.

MRS. KLEIN. Glasses. Glasses. Say I'm ready. Take the bags out.

PAULA *goes out.* MRS. KLEIN *finds her glasses.*

Keys.

She takes a large bunch of keys out of her handbag. Locks the drinks cabinet. Finds Dr. Schmideberg's letter; puts it in the filing cabinet. At some point the taxi driver hoots his horn. MRS. KLEIN *puts the keys in the bookshelf and selects a book to hide them behind. One last look round. She goes out.*

PAULA *comes back. Puts on a light, draws the curtains. Sits at the desk, moves things round to find a working order. Starts work.*

Music.

Time passes.

Some hours later.

PAULA *is still working.*

Front door heard opening and closing.

PAULA. Hello?

MELITTA *comes in.*

MELITTA. What the bloody hell are you doing here?

PAULA. I'm reading proofs.

MELITTA. What for?

PAULA. She asked me to.

MELITTA. When?

PAULA. This afternoon.

MELITTA. She wasn't here this afternoon.

PAULA. I saw her.

MELITTA. Here?

PAULA. Yes here.

MELITTA. Oh Jesus Christ.

PAULA. What is it?

MELITTA. Nothing.

PAULA. Would you like some coffee?

MELITTA. No. I need a drink. And you?

PAULA. I'm not thirsty.

MELITTA. Never stopped *me.*

Tries the drinks cupboard.

It's locked.

PAULA. Let me try it.

Does.

That's strange.

Tries again.

It is. I'm sorry.

MELITTA. Darling it's not your fault. You carry on.

PAULA. I will. Did that sound rude? She wants them done by Wednesday and it's taken me four hours to do one chapter.

Pause. MELITTA *moves around the room.*

MELITTA. Aren't you freezing?

PAULA. No.

MELITTA. Why don't you put the heating on?

PAULA. I tried. It didn't light and I was worried I might break it so I left it. Let me finish.

Pause. MELITTA *looks over* PAULA*'s shoulder at her work.*

MELITTA. I'm in this.

PAULA. I know, I've just been doing the footnote.

MELITTA. And that's not an ashtray.

PAULA. No?

MELITTA. It's part of a coffee-set.

Replaces saucer with ashtray.

Here.

Empties stubs, moves around, stacks sherry glasses and generally tidies up.

PAULA. Are you here for something special?

MELITTA. No, I happened to be driving past and saw the light on. Someone's moved a book.

PAULA. Not me.

MELITTA. So let me get this straight, you saw her here this afternoon.

PAULA. That's right.

MELITTA. Because she should have left on Tuesday.

PAULA. No, she left as planned. I'm sure of that. Because when Walter rang me – .

MELITTA. *Walter* rang you?

PAULA. Yes, he – .

MELITTA. Why?

PAULA. He had a message. That she wanted me to call on her. She'd got my letter and she – .

MELITTA. Letter?

PAULA. Yes. I wrote a letter. Everyone else was writing to her. I assumed you wouldn't mind.

MELITTA. Why should I mind?

PAULA. I mean, I didn't think *she'd* mind.

MELITTA. And so the sequence was: you wrote a letter to my mother and she sent an invitation via my husband. That's what happened.

PAULA. That's what happened.

MELITTA. And?

PAULA. She asked me if I'd – .

MELITTA. No not you.

PAULA. Your mother?

MELITTA. Yes my mother. How did she seem?

PAULA *tidies her papers for an orderly start next day.*

PAULA. Her dreams have stopped, I don't know if she told you. And she cries from time to time but the tears don't help. She's still denying the loss. Is this what you want to know, I don't – ?

MELITTA. Go on.

PAULA. She's trying to re-instate the lost loved object: keeping Hans's letters in a place of safety. Tearing other papers up, because she sees them perhaps as hostile. She has periods of elation. And of deep depression. She's in mourning.

MELITTA. Did she mention me?

PAULA. She said you had the car.

MELITTA. What else?

PAULA. I don't remember.

MELITTA. You're a liar.

PAULA. That may be. I can't discuss it, not at this time of night. I'm sorry Melitta.

She goes out. MELITTA *tries to open top drawer of filing cabinet. Locked. Goes to desk, rummages round in top drawers. Finds only pins, elastic bands, etc. Moves away.* PAULA *comes back wearing a hat and coat.*

MELITTA. You've got your coat on.

PAULA. Yes. It's late, I'll miss my Underground.

MELITTA. I'll drive you home.

PAULA. What for?

MELITTA. Oh don't you want me to?

PAULA. I'd love you to. I hate the tube. It's full of drunks and madmen. But it just so happens that through no decision of my own I live the other end of London.

MELITTA. But I've got the car.

PAULA. I'll pay for the petrol.

MELITTA. Rubbish, you can't afford it.

PAULA. Fine. Let's go.

MELITTA. Let's stay for a moment.

PAULA. Not too long. I'm tired. (*Her eyes are strained.*) I have to check each word. Although she's changing nothing essential. Misprints. Extra foot- notes. Foreword. Brand new chapter. (*Laughs.*) Quite a lot in fact but nothing essential.

MELITTA. So you're doing her secretarial work?

PAULA. Not really.

MELITTA. And her letters, will you file her letters?

PAULA. No.

MELITTA. Although they're streaming in in sackfuls, so it seems.

PAULA. They won't need filing.

MELITTA. So you'll put them where?

PAULA. In here. (*Basket.*) The filing cabinet's locked.

MELITTA. Well that's a bore. She asked me to collect some papers. But I don't know where the keys are.

PAULA. I don't know.

MELITTA. Well somebody must.

PAULA. The cleaning woman knows. They had an arrangement, hide them – somewhere in the house, I don't know where, it's not my business.

Pause.

Most of the house is locked. She's locked the cellar door, she's locked the rooms upstairs. It's symbolic. The house is her.

Pause. PAULA *smiles.*

Let's go.

MELITTA. When I was briefly – fairly briefly – couple of months – or less – prevailed upon to be her private secretary – I threw a vase and hit that bit of wall behind you.

PAULA. I'm reading proofs. Which suits me fine. I don't like. weekends at the best of times, they're lonely and depressing so I don't mind helping. But I'm not her secretary, I'm not her anything else, let's make that clear.

MELITTA *looks up a number in her address book.*

MELITTA. There's a fascinating paper by Ferenczi on neurotic weekends. He says that during the week our work routine soaks up aggressive feelings. Here we are.

Finds number. Dials.

But then at weekends they let fly. You follow? That's why Sunday is the day we dread the most. Pandora's box stuffed full of nameless hatreds. And the lid not properly closed. (*To telephone:*) Oh bloody answer. Stupid savages. Hello. Oh thank you, can I speak to Mrs. P? (*To herself:*) Oh Bugger. Pow. Pownall. (*Into telephone:*) Mrs. Pountney. Phew. Yes this is Dr. Schmideberg speaking. S.C.H – . Doctor, that's right. No, no-one's ill, I simply – . (*To* PAULA *in comic cockney:*) 'Gawn to fetch 'er 'usband.' Hello. This is – . No, there's nothing wrong, I have your name down here in my address-book as an avenue to Mrs. Pountney, I believe she lives on the floor above you. Yes I do, it's twenty to eleven.

PAULA. Melitta.

MELITTA *in fury bangs the telephone on the desk.*

MELITTA. I'm sorry, I dropped the phone. That's very kind, if you could have a look, that's right. Tell her it's Melitta. She knows me, yes, she very kindly cleans my mother's house for her. Tell her I'm there, I'm here, and everything's locked up and ask her where the keys are. No there isn't any need to – . (*To* PAULA:) Now he's putting his wife back on.

PAULA. Melitta.

MELITTA. What.

PAULA. She's gone away for the weekend.

MELITTA. Mrs. Pountney?

PAULA nods.

MELITTA (*to telephone*). One moment please. (*To* PAULA :) Has she gone far?

PAULA. To South – . South something.

MELITTA. Southport? Southsea?

PAULA. No, it's something anal.

MELITTA. Southend.

PAULA. That sounds right.

Worried voice on telephone: 'Hello? Has somebody passed away? Hello?'

MELITTA. Thank you, I've just found out. Good night.

Rings off.

Damn that woman. Damn her. God rot her to hell. Vile crone. I've begged my mother a thousand times to sack her. But she won't. She can't. She sees the cleaning-woman as her mother. Wouldn't you say?

PAULA. It crossed my mind, Melitta, but I didn't like to call attention to it. Can we go now?

MELITTA. Did she get my letter?

PAULA. Yes.

MELITTA. And did she read it?

PAULA. Not while I was there. She said you'd marked it to await return. No, let's be frank. She felt attacked by it. She's feeling persecuted at the moment, or she'd know you wouldn't hurt her at a time like – . But she feared you might. So she was hostile to the letter and to you. But not you, her daughter. No. To Dr. Schmideberg. She only spoke of you as Dr. Schmideberg. The daughter's good, she loves her, but the doctor's bad, it's casebook stuff. It won't last. She'll read your letter soon. In fact she probably took it with her.

MELITTA. Jesus Christ.

PAULA. What now?

MELITTA. I'm feeling sick.

PAULA. Do you want a glass of water?

MELITTA. No.

PAULA. Try putting your head between your knees.

MELITTA. I need a drink.

PAULA. Let's see what we can do.

Goes to the drinks cabinet. Examines it. Takes out the top drawer.

I thought so.

Reaches down inside.

One can always find a way in somehow, as my professor would say.

Gets bottles and glasses out.

Whisky? There's two kinds. Oh this is Irish. Irish Scotch, that's rather amusing.

MELITTA. Pour it.

PAULA. Yes I am doing.

MELITTA. One for you.

PAULA. I have.

They drink.

PAULA. I bought a whisky once in a public house. In Bethnal Green. But it was such a noisy and disgusting place I couldn't enjoy it. This is different. This is homelike.

Pause.

MELITTA. Do you have those dreams where something absolutely vital has been hidden away? In some familiar place? You search and search. But the handles keep on coming off the doors. Or empty rooms are suddenly crowded. Or the railway-ticket's missing from your handbag, or the platform's vanished. And you can't admit whatever it is you're doing. Because it's shameful. Do you?

PAULA. Not the same but – . Yes.

MELITTA. It's not just me then.

PAULA. They're anxiety dreams. Everyone has them.

MELITTA. I feel I'm in one all the time.

PAULA. I dream I've killed a child. I told my analyst. She interpreted that I'd felt deserted by her over the Easter break. I said I doubted that was much to do with it, I'd been having this dream for thirty years. She said, 'Ah ha, and my consulting-room is number 30.'

MELITTA. Are we like that?

PAULA. I hope not. What about yours?

MELITTA. She wasn't giving satisfaction so I sacked her.

PAULA. What went wrong?

MELITTA. I thought she was my mother. And I couldn't work through it. Couldn't stop thinking, 'damn the bitch', or 'does she love me?'. So she thought, and I agreed, that I was stuck in the transference. I'm a sucker for transference. Can't resist it. Do it to anyone. Dentist. Window-cleaner. Nanki Poo. So on we slogged. For years and years. And nothing changed. Except that bit by bit I realised that to all intents and purposes she *was* my mother. It was my mother put me on to her. She reads my mother's books, she quotes them word for word and once a month she meets her for tea at Whiteleys. And I couldn't bear it, darling.

PAULA. Who've you gone to now?

MELITTA. Never you mind.

PAULA. I'd like to change my analyst.

MELITTA. Who do you have your eye on?

PAULA. Well it's more a question would she take me.

MELITTA *spills her whisky. Composes herself. Marks a level on the glass with one finger.*

MELITTA. Be a good girl and fill it up to *here* this time.

PAULA *does. She looks at the bottle.*

PAULA. It's seven years old. She must be quite a connoisseur.

MELITTA. She is. We drove through France two years ago and just as we were getting on quite well she went in for a claret tasting competition and won first prize. They'd never had a woman champion. Now the mayor sends her a postcard every Christmas. She's a local hero.

PAULA *smiles.*

It isn't funny, being her daughter. Try it. Perhaps you have.

PAULA. I don't know what you mean.

MELITTA. You've changed.

PAULA. How's that?

MELITTA. You're like some stubborn, slow amoeba making its gains by stealth.

PAULA *goes to the pin-box and rummages for her five shillings.*

Just what do you think you're doing?

PAULA. I'm getting a taxi.

MELITTA. Put that back.

PAULA. It's my expenses.

MELITTA. Well you might have told me you had taxi-money.

PAULA. I forgot.

MELITTA. Forgot. You didn't want to leave. You're burrowing in.

PAULA *throws the box on the ground. It opens and the money falls out.*

PAULA. I have a mother of my own. I don't need yours. If that's the undercurrent. Why do you think I'd want to hurt you? Why? You're like a sister to me. You've been kind and good and generous to me. Nobody else from home has helped me. Not till now. Until your mother, true. Who seems neurotically attached to me for some strange reason. Or some obvious reason. I can't help it. And I'm under no illusions. And I don't care tuppence for your boring little Oedipal tangles. I have other problems thank you. I've a daughter in Berlin, I have consulting-rooms in Bethnal Green.

MELITTA. Who put you there?

PAULA. Not her.

MELITTA. They all did. At the Institute. Committee level. Refugees not wanted. Not in Hampstead. Too much healthy competition. That's why they've dumped you all in these extraordinary places. And she's right behind it.

PAULA. You don't surprise me. Analysts are only human. If you threaten our professional livelihoods you'll get some very primitive responses. That was grubby of you.

MELITTA. Did she tell you how he died?

PAULA. She said a climbing accident.

MELITTA. He killed himself.

Pause.

PAULA. How do you know?

MELITTA. I rang my aunt. Auntie Jolan. Mrs. Vago. Talks for ever, cost a fortune. I could tell at once that she was hiding something. So I asked her very obliquely. Where he went that morning. What he wore. All the little details that I needed to complete the picture. She resisted. Started howling. Then she banged the phone down. But I'd got my answers. I've got good material. And I've worked it through. I've reached the only possible interpretation.

PAULA. Did he leave a note?

MELITTA. No note. That's what he was like. He used to disappear for hours. She'd shake him. 'Where've you been? I thought the cart had run you over!' He'd say: 'Nowhere.' Never let on. Though he might give her a clue. But no confessions. So he'd hardly leave a suicide-note. He wouldn't want to give her the satisfaction.

PAULA. Does your mother know?

MELITTA. Well that depends on whether or not she read my letter.

PAULA. Oh Melitta. She'll be – .

MELITTA. Yes I know.

PAULA. You told her?

MELITTA. Yes!

PAULA. It's horrible.

MELITTA. Yes I know.

PAULA. How could you?

MELITTA. Well I think I must be barmy.

Another drink for both.

MELITTA. When you saw it, where was it left exactly?

PAULA. There. (*The desk.*) It's gone now.

MELITTA. Yes I looked.

Pause.

PAULA. I'm starving.

MELITTA. Likewise.

Pause.

PAULA. Was the letter very – ?

MELITTA. Very detailed. Very convincing. Very persecutorily sadistic.

PAULA. Oh my God.

MELITTA. Exactly.

Pause.

MELITTA. I was sitting in the Wigmore Hall tonight. And they were playing Schubert. So divine. And all that horrible hatred seeped away. I felt that I was looking at it from high up. From somewhere in the ceiling. It was like a pile of rotting clothes. Far distant. From my dizzy height of rational thinking. I felt utterly sane. So I came round here to get my letter back. It seemed so simple. Now all I can imagine is my mother in her first class Pullman, looking for some further reading, putting down her copy of the Psychoanalytic Quarterly – .

She laughs.

PAULA. No, Melitta –

MELITTA. No. Or maybe her Country Life –

PAULA. Or Vogue!

They both giggle.

MELITTA. Or Lilliput!

Both giggle hysterically.

MELITTA. She'll climb into bed –

PAULA. No, berth!

MELITTA. What?

PAULA. Berth, you know, the – .

MELITTA. Berth, that's right, she'll take her corsets off –

Both giggle furiously.

– then up she climbs and –

PAULA. – does her nightie up to her chin –

Both collapse with laughter.

MELITTA. And then she reads – she reads –

PAULA. 'You cow, you murderess – '

MELITTA. No no no – it's worse that that – .

PAULA. 'Bitch, you killed him – !'

They slowly stop giggling. Then one of them starts giggling again, and both collapse with laughter but this time with a sense of guilt. They stop.

Pause. They share a handkerchief, wipe their eyes.

Maybe she won't believe it.

MELITTA. She's not stupid.

PAULA. No.

MELITTA. It'll kill her.

PAULA. Yes it very likely will.

MELITTA. Except she could have left it here. It could be in this room.

They gaze round the room.

PAULA. What was the book you thought I'd moved?

MELITTA. 'The Interpretation of Dreams'.

PAULA stands up.

PAULA. That seems significant.

Goes to the bookshelf. Removes the book and takes the keys out.

I thought so. Catch.

She throws them across the room. MELITTA catches them.

PAULA. Have a look.

MELITTA opens the filing cabinet.

MELITTA. You keep watch.

PAULA. Who for?

MELITTA. Parental super-egos, darling. Do it.

She unlocks the filing cabinet.

PAULA (*whispers*). Go on.

MELITTA opens the top drawer to its fullest extent. The cabinet topples forwards into her arms. She struggles to push it back. PAULA runs to help her.

MRS. KLEIN comes in, dressed for travel as last seen.

MRS. KLEIN. Melitta?

MELITTA. Mother?

MRS. KLEIN. Paula, you're a big strong girl, if you could help the taxi-fellow.

PAULA *goes out.*

MRS. KLEIN. So: I'm back.

MELITTA. What happened?

MRS. KLEIN. Aren't you pleased to see me? Give your mother a kiss.

They kiss.

MRS. KLEIN. Look in your handbag, I've no money, only marks and travellers' cheques.

MELITTA *does.*

It's wonderful you're here my darling. Stay the night. Your room's the same. I've kept it as it was. Some books are new, some boxes, half a billiard-table, as a matter of fact it's packed with rubbish. Stay.

PAULA *comes in with luggage.*

PAULA. One more bag to come. He wants his fare.

MRS. KLEIN. I'm not surprised, he's just got married. To a nice Irish girl, he tells me, and they have some minor sexual problems but I think I've helped him. (*To* MELITTA .) How're we doing?

MELITTA. I've got a shilling.

MRS. KLEIN. That's no good, the fare is four and ninepence.

MELITTA. Paula's got some money, haven't you Paula?

MRS. KLEIN. Thank you Paula.

PAULA *crouches and looks round the floor for the money from the pinbox.*

PAULA. Sorry it must have rolled.

MRS. KLEIN (*to* MELITTA). What's she up to?

PAULA. Got it.

MRS. KLEIN. Quite a party you've been having.

PAULA *gives her the two half-crowns.* MRS. KLEIN *takes more money off* MELITTA.

MRS. KLEIN. Sixpence for the tip, that's five and thruppence. Off you go now.

PAULA *goes.*

MELITTA. Did you get my letter?

MRS. KLEIN. Later. What's she doing here?

MELITTA. Working late.

MRS. KLEIN. I wish she'd go. She found the keys I notice. And the whisky. Make me a cup of tea. I need to make a note of something, personal, not unpleasant. Turn the heating on.

MELITTA *goes out.* MRS. KLEIN *gets her notebook. Loosens her shoes. Takes hat off.* MRS. KLEIN *puts a record on. Slow movement, Haydn, Quartet in C, Op. 54 No. 2.*

Interlude

Not very long but marks a pause longer than a usual dip in the action. MRS. KLEIN *makes notes. Listens to the music, cries. Wipes her eyes, shakes her head. Makes more notes. At some point* PAULA *comes in with a suitcase.*

MRS. KLEIN. I'm working.

PAULA *puts it down quietly and goes out.*

MELITTA *comes in with a tray of tea-things.*

End of Interlude

MELITTA. Paula's sitting in the hall.

MRS. KLEIN. At least she's quiet.

MELITTA. Be nice to her.

MRS. KLEIN *goes to the door and calls through it.*

MRS. KLEIN. Paula, we've got an extra cup. Come in for a moment.

PAULA *does. They all sit.*

MRS. KLEIN. Now who is to be mother?

MELITTA. That's your job.

MRS. KLEIN. Do it! Paula has an Underground to catch.

MELITTA. She missed it hours ago.

MRS. KLEIN. So how's she getting home?

MELITTA. I'm driving her.

MRS. KLEIN. You can't, you're sozzled.

MELITTA. I am not!

MRS. KLEIN. I'm teasing you, my darling. Pour the tea.

MELITTA *pours tea.*

MRS. KLEIN. That's my girl. I've earned my rest. I am exhausted. But euphoric. Something wonderful has happened. Dover station. In the buffet, where I ate a cheese and pickle sandwich, quite disgusting, first I dozed and then I fell asleep. A wooden bench. A lucky bench because I dreamt on it.

She pauses, takes MELITTA*'s hand.*

I know this tea, it's kitchen tea, it comes from Mrs. Pountney's caddy, it's the nicest cup of tea I've ever tasted.

I saw a mother and her son. The son had either died or was about to die. The mother was dressed in black, her collar was white. I didn't feel sad to see them. I felt slightly hostile. So: I woke. And saw the boat-train just about to leave for London so I took it.

MELITTA. What about the boat?

MRS. KLEIN. The boat had left.

MELITTA. You missed it?

MRS. KLEIN. I decided not to take it.

PAULA. You resisted it?

MRS. KLEIN. Paula, look in the fridge, you'll find some nice salami.

PAULA *goes.*

MRS. KLEIN. I didn't like to say while she was here. It struck me just in time that I could not attend the funeral for an obvious reason.

MELITTA. What?

MRS. KLEIN. I might have met your father.

MELITTA. And?

MRS. KLEIN. He might have propositioned me.

MELITTA *breaks into surprised laughter.*

MRS. KLEIN. No good?

MELITTA. No good. Besides he's married.

MRS. KLEIN. Not that *that* would – . No you're right. There's something deeper. Deep resistance. Do me a favour, don't tell her. How long's she staying?

MELITTA. As long as I do.

PAULA comes in with salami, plates and a knife.

MRS. KLEIN. Paula you're staying the night. (*To* MELITTA.) Now where's she sleeping?

MELITTA. Sofa.

MRS. KLEIN (*to* PAULA). Sofa.

MELITTA (*this is a routine they used to do in the past*). So: this mother?

MRS. KLEIN. So this mother. Mother and son. A dying son.

MELITTA. Or dead.

MRS. KLEIN. Who told you dead?

MELITTA. Look at your notes.

MRS. KLEIN. No I believe you. But he wasn't Hans. Because the mother wasn't me. Because I felt hostility towards her. So I – .

PAULA. What about the dress?

MRS. KLEIN. Too much prompting. Find the salami. Dress, a dress, quite right, black dress white collar which I – . Which I'm wearing at this moment. So: a hint of my unconscious knowledge that it's I who is bereaved. So my denial is weakened. Only slightly. Quite a long way to go. (*Sees the salami.*) You found it, thank you.

Starts cutting it up.

In my childhood, in the summer, we would go on picnics. All the family. And my father used to sit on a stump and say to me: 'Melchen, darling, here's a nice thin piece of salami'. And he'd cut it.

She gives a thin piece to PAULA.

MRS. KLEIN. And he'd give it to me. Then he'd turn to my older sister, and he'd say: 'And now a nice thick slice of salami for my favourite daughter'.

She gives a thick piece to MELITTA. *Cuts more salami and gives it all to* MELITTA.

Now this, Melitta, was a learned man, a student of the Talmud, what was called a bocher, spoke in German, English, Slovak, French, he learned from some old chap who fought at the battle of Waterloo. And yet, unthinkingly, he stirred up envy in me.

PAULA (*wanting another piece of salami*). Could I –.

MRS. KLEIN. – have a bath, of course.

MELITTA. It won't be hot yet.

MRS. KLEIN. True, it will be cool and healthy. (*To* MELITTA). Run the taps.

PAULA. I'd rather –.

MRS. KLEIN. Fine, you do it yourself.

PAULA. I wonder if you'd mind if –.

MRS. KLEIN. Bathtime.

Goes out, leaving MRS. KLEIN *and* MELITTA *eating salami.*

MELITTA. Did you take my – ?

MRS. KLEIN. Have children.

MELITTA. Mother.

MRS. KLEIN. I'm broody. I want to be a nice warm bobba. I want to smell of cooking-oil and make-up. I want enormous corseted hips for little boys to throw their arms round.

MELITTA. Did you read my letter?

MRS. KLEIN. No.

MELITTA. I guessed you hadn't.

MRS. KLEIN. I'm sorry.

MELITTA. If you give it back I'll write you an up-to-date one.

MRS. KLEIN *gives* MELITTA *the keys and indicates the filing cabinet.*

MRS. KLEIN. Bottom drawer.

MELITTA *looks for her letter and finds it.*

MRS. KLEIN. The middle drawer contains my dealings with the world. It is my ego drawer. The top drawer is my super-ego drawer, it's full of tax reminders, bills for the rates, all those harsh commands which come from up on high. The bottom drawer is dark and filled with menace.

MELITTA. You put my letter in your id drawer!

MRS. KLEIN. Yes, who cares. Don't stand there like an idiot, darling, sit beside me.

MELITTA. Shouldn't I make the beds up?

MRS. KLEIN. They can wait.

MELITTA. She'll need a towel.

MRS. KLEIN. She'll find one. No, I locked them up. I locked the soap up. You should have seen me more these last few days. You missed some fine old symptoms. Sit.

MELITTA does.

MRS KLEIN. That's better.

Pause.

MRS. KLEIN. In a moment, in the fridge, you'll find some nice Gewürztraminer. It's a smoky wine, it goes with what we're eating.

MELITTA. Fine.

MRS. KLEIN (*of the letter*). What's in that letter?

MELITTA. Paula tells me you were hostile towards it.

MRS. KLEIN. I thought you were attacking my criminality paper. Quite absurd. I saw the address and – . Let me see it.

MELITTA hands it to her.

MRS. KLEIN. Yes, it was the way you'd underlined the 'Mrs'. *Mrs* Klein. Like you're the learned doctor, I'm the uppity layman.

MELITTA. Show me.

MRS. KLEIN *gives it to her.*

MELITTA. That's a smudge.

MRS KLEIN *takes it back. Looks.*

MRS. KLEIN. So who did this?

MELITTA. The postman probably.

MRS. KLEIN *puts glasses on, looks harder.*

MRS. KLEIN. There you are, I had a persecutory delusion. I felt my little torch of knowledge was being crapped on yet again, you'll pardon me, that's what it feels like when it happens. Though it isn't you I blame, my darling. Glover's the worst.

She slices off a piece of salami.

MELITTA. You mean the wurst.

MRS. KLEIN. The wurst, that's right. Yes, Glover's the wurst.

Playfully stabs the salami. Laughs.

Somebody told me Edward Glover took his Easter holiday inside a cloud. Right in one. With his wife and little backward daughter, whom he loves and takes wherever he goes, despite, or possibly because of her condition. So. They went to Scotland. Up a mountain. Right to the top. Set up camp and then the mist descended. So they couldn't leave their tent. But Edward Glover stuck to plan and stayed there for a fortnight, while his wife and daughter begged for mercy. Finally he upped their pegs and down the slope they walked and not a quarter of a mile below are sunny fields and rippling brooks and people in their bathing costumes. The weather was fine, there was a tiny cloud up *there*, that's all, and in his boring daddy's dogmatism he had spent his holiday inside it.

MELITTA *laughs.*

MRS. KLEIN. Perhaps you see less of him these days?

MELITTA. Rather more.

Pause.

MRS. KLEIN. You *will* attack my criminality paper.

MELITTA. Probably. Yes.

MRS. KLEIN. In the Journal?

MELITTA. Probably in the Journal. In the Journal.

MRS. KLEIN (*suddenly angry*). Why do you do this?

Pause.

What I write, I've learned and proved in twenty years of clinical practice. And you've seen the results.

MELITTA. I have. You're a great clinician. But Mother, you can't write rubbish and expect me not to say it's rubbish.

MRS. KLEIN. No I don't, because I know you see the so-called rubbish, 'dreck' you called it once, the *poisonous faeces*, aimed at you in person. I can see it, everyone else can see it. It's an embarrassment. Why exhibit your sores in public, darling?

MELITTA. Sores?

MRS. KLEIN. Yes sores, emotional sores. If I fought back you'd see some dreck all right. I could finish your career. Only I won't attack my daughter.

MELITTA (*suddenly angry, shouts*). No, you get your little toadies to attack your daughter.

MRS. KLEIN. I don't write papers for my fellow thinkers.

MELITTA. You'll do anything to win. You'll pack committees, you'll fiddle agendas, you'll steal other people's patients.

MRS. KLEIN. When did I steal a patient? Whose damn patient?

MELITTA. Mine last month.

MRS. KLEIN. He begged for refuge. You'd confused him. You're a bad clinician.

MELITTA. Why?

MRS. KLEIN. You want the truth? Good, fine. You reassure your patients. When they cry you hug them. And you say their clouds have silver linings and you give them tips on life. What can they learn from that about themselves? All they learn is that you're nice to them, which as a matter of fact you aren't, you're bloody destructive.

Take that patient. All his life, like everyone else, like you, like me, like all the world, he has projected his infant experiences on to the people around him. But it's only now, with me, he starts to see them. Now, in that powerful, terrifying thing we call the transference. Because, unlike his wife or child or *you*, I am detached. So the *screen*, as it were, is blank. And he projects and sees, *on me*, those images from his cradle. You obscured that screen with your emotions. You felt pity. And you felt protective. Rubbish. Dreck, dreck, dreck. If you want to be an analyst of any worth you have to trust your patients with the truth. However harsh. They're strong. They'll take it.

MELITTA *gives her her letter.*

MRS. KLEIN. What is it?

MELITTA. It's the truth about Hans.

Goes out.

End of Act One

ACT TWO

Later.

MRS. KLEIN *and* PAULA. PAULA *is on the sofa.*

MELITTA *'s letter, unopened. A bottle of wine.*

Pause.

MRS. KLEIN. Where's Paula?

PAULA. I'm Paula. Melitta's upstairs. She's having a bath.

MRS. KLEIN *pours wine for them both.*

MRS. KLEIN. I've had two great depressions in my life. One when I was an angry housewife. One in Berlin when nobody paid enough attention to me. Now number three is looming. I can see it. Like a thick black line just over my field of vision.

She opens MELITTA *'s letter. Glances at a page.*

Should I read Melitta's letter?

PAULA. Perhaps not now.

MRS. KLEIN. Quite right.

She tears it up. Throws the bits of paper in the waste-paper-basket.

Pause.

Deep depression.

Pause.

MRS. KLEIN. So: my dream.

PAULA. Your mother and son.

MRS. KLEIN. *This* mother and son. And the associations ran as follows. Picnic, father, sibling envy, Battle of Waterloo. That's hopeless. Battle of – .

Pause.

Homework. I think I'm getting somewhere. Brother's homework.

Pause.

There is a nasty woman comes to mind who brought her equally nasty son to help my brother with his homework. I was twelve. It seems to me that mother and son was them.

PAULA. Why dream about them now?

MRS. KLEIN. Because I never forgot that evening. It was horrible, frightful. Everybody was upset. My mother was in tears, my brother rushed into his room and slammed the door, I could have killed them both.

PAULA. For being upset?

MRS. KLEIN. Because they – . No, not *them*. This woman and – .

She registers the misunderstanding.

I *thought* it was –.

Ponders the implications.

I'm feeling worse now. Like the ceiling's getting lower. Say something, anything.

PAULA. I have a dream in which the ceiling's getting lower.

MRS. KLEIN. Tell me, it can't be worse than what's going on up here.

PAULA. There's a small girl. But she's older than me. She's moving her dolls round the floor. She makes me feel uneasy. And the roof keeps sinking. Suddenly a little door flies open and she – .

MRS. KLEIN. Ssh. She's coming down.

MELITTA *comes in carrying bedclothes.*

MELITTA. I've come to say good night. If we're still talking to each other.

MRS. KLEIN. We're still talking.

MELITTA. Did you open it this time?

MRS. KLEIN. Yes I did.

MELITTA. And how do you feel?

MRS. KLEIN. I feel severe depression coming on, but I'll survive it.

MELITTA. Good. I mean, that you'll survive it.

MRS. KLEIN. I'll survive it.

MELITTA. No hard feelings?

MRS. KLEIN. Not on a conscious level.

MELITTA. I was sitting in the Wigmore Hall tonight and thought about it and I – .

MRS. KLEIN. Let's not talk about it now. All right?

MELITTA. All right.

MRS. KLEIN. And so.

MELITTA. And so. Did you really mean to get there?

MRS. KLEIN. Where?

MELITTA. To Budapest.

MRS. KLEIN. It seems unlikely.

MELITTA. But you would have done. If I'd gone with you. If I'd dragged you.

MRS. KLEIN. If you'd dragged me, yes I might have.

MELITTA (*to* PAULA). We used to live in a flat quite near the castle. Big tall shutters. Always dark inside. (*To her mother.*) We could have gone to see it. We could have gone to the Hotel Gellert for coffee and cakes. I could have cheered you up.

MRS. KLEIN. That's not your *métier*.

Pause.

MELITTA (*to* PAULA). Two sheets. Three blankets. Say if you want an extra pillow. Would you rather sleep upstairs?

PAULA. The couch is fine.

MELITTA. The sofa.

PAULA. What?

MELITTA. The couch comes next week. Or haven't you asked her yet?

MRS. KLEIN. If you mean that Paula wants to be my patient, I had guessed as much. She'll ask me in her own good time and I'll consider it then. Good night.

MELITTA. Good night.

PAULA. Good night.

MRS. KLEIN. Melitta.

MELITTA. Yes?

MRS. KLEIN. Don't turn the heating off.

MELITTA. I wasn't going to. 'Night.

She goes.

PAULA. That was tactless of her.

MRS. KLEIN. She'll be back.

MELITTA *comes back in.*

MELITTA. What about my letter?

MRS. KLEIN. It's the middle of the night for God's sake. I've been travelling. I'm depressed. I'm in mourning.

MELITTA. So am I.

MRS. KLEIN. So what do you want, to bully me about it? Give me time.

MELITTA. We'll talk about it over breakfast.

MRS. KLEIN. Maybe.

PAULA. If she doesn't want to read it then she shouldn't have to.

MELITTA. If she – .

MRS. KLEIN. *That* was tactless.

MELITTA. But she said she had. She said – .

MRS. KLEIN. If I may clarify? I opened it and Paula told me not to read it so I tore it up. Omnipotence. I'm doing a lot of it. I was interpreting my dream just now and Paula led me to an obvious breakthrough and I wouldn't listen.

MELITTA. Tore it up?

MRS. KLEIN. I wouldn't listen! Something's being resisted.

MELITTA. Yes it is!

MRS. KLEIN. But what?

MELITTA. I'll tell you.

MRS. KLEIN. Good, you tell me. Well?

PAULA. I'll go upstairs.

MRS. KLEIN. I want you here.

MELITTA. Why can't we talk about it just we two?

MRS. KLEIN. Because there's no such thing as just we two. There's always a third. At least a third. The mother. Perhaps the father, perhaps a rival sibling. Always the room fills up. Start with two, why not with three? Either way we'll end up throwing a party. Good, let's start.

MELITTA. Last Friday Hans was – .

MRS. KLEIN. In your opinion Hans's death was not what it appeared. I read that far.

MELITTA. He left the – .

MRS. KLEIN. Then the ceiling started moving so I stopped.

MELITTA. Mother, listen.

MRS. KLEIN. Yes? Go on. Go on.

MELITTA. Last Friday Hans left the boarding-house where he was staying in Rosenberg.

MRS. KLEIN. Not Rosenberg my dear. You're stuck in the past. It was Rosenberg when you and he lived there as children. After the war the name was changed. It's called Ruzomberok. Which means the same. One moment please.

She pauses and puts her hand over her eyes.

Now I feel as though I'm wearing an eyeshade. Well?

MELITTA. He left the boarding-house – .

MRS. KLEIN. You think of it as Rosenberg because the name evokes a time of primitive content. Before all this. My presence gave you warmth and comfort.

MELITTA. You were hardly ever there.

MRS. KLEIN. I wasn't well. And so the doctor did what doctors do, prescribed a holiday and then another, then a rest-cure and they all joined up.

MELITTA *laughs.*

And you were cared for by your bobba. Who was God's own housewife. She was a saint on earth as long as she was not one's mother. That was my little problem and I failed to solve it and I got depressed.

MELITTA. You could have written.

MRS. KLEIN. The way I felt I'd have depressed you too.

MELITTA. You missed my birthday.

MRS. KLEIN. Oh, so now we're get to the momentous crisis. I missed your birthday and you're scarred for life.

MELITTA. I am. Not just –

MRS. KLEIN. And maybe the cat jumped on your cradle so now you can't drink milk. Melitta that is popular psychiatry, it's rubbish, it's for chambermaids. So you had a bad experience, rise above it. Take it to your analyst, she's good, I like her. Where'd we got to. Yes: he left the boarding-house and – . Let me tell you something. I would walk you to the square. And find a bench. When you were five or six, a difficult age, and Hans was three. I'd buy you ice-creams and I'd introduce you to the pigeons. And I'd watch the fountain. And I'd sit and wait to go back home where mother would have staked her claim to Jewish motherhood by cooking a five-course dinner. And I'd feel despair. That this was it. My life. My waste of life. So I escaped. And don't think you've got cause to feel resentful. You've a doctorship, a fine career and if you choose to throw it away that's your decision. Now: he travelled to the mountains. How?

MELITTA. He took the bus. He bought a single ticket.

MRS. KLEIN. No that doesn't make sense. To get the special rate you buy two tickets, one to get there, one to – . Has the system changed?

MELITTA. He wasn't coming back.

MRS. KLEIN. I'm confused. Paula, explain.

PAULA. He – .

MELITTA. Mother, what do you think I'm trying to tell you?

MRS. KLEIN. What?

Pause.

You mean he – ?

Pause.

And this is how you spring it on me?

MELITTA. Mother – .

MRS. KLEIN. Let me say: his recent letters gave no cause for worry

He was well and happy. Two weeks ago he wrote to tell me all about a Cossack costume which he'd put together for a party. Boots from somebody at work, the hat from – . Two whole pages. Quite a tedious letter. But it doesn't seem a likely one from someone who's about to kill himself.

MELITTA. He was – .

MRS. KLEIN. Wait, wait, wait. How do you know he only bought a single ticket?

MELITTA. The return half wasn't in his pockets.

MRS. KLEIN. How do you know?

MELITTA. Aunt Jolan searched them.

MRS. KLEIN. And you rang her up? *That* says something.

MELITTA. Can I go on?

MRS. KLEIN. I'm here, I have no patients waiting.

MELITTA. Only Paula.

MRS. KLEIN. Paula's listening, Paula's fine. Continue.

MELITTA. He was wearing ordinary weekday shoes, not climbing boots.

MRS. KLEIN. I hear you.

MELITTA. He'd taken nothing to read.

PAULA. This is ridiculous.

MRS. KLEIN. Let her go on. She needs it. Well?

MELITTA. He took nothing to eat.

MRS. KLEIN. So there's a restaurant in the mountains.

MELITTA. He ate breakfast there. He left a tip. He gave the waiter all his change. He'd nothing left.

MRS. KLEIN. No banknotes?

MELITTA. No.

MRS. KLEIN. His wallet?

MELITTA. Empty.

PAULA. They could have robbed the body.

MRS. KLEIN. I hadn't visualised him as a – . It might be better if you keep your comments to yourself. (*To* MELITTA:) Go on.

MELITTA. They found him at the foot of the cliff which looks back over Ruzomberok.

MRS. KLEIN. Ah.

MELITTA. Do you know it?

MRS. KLEIN. No, I – . No.

MELITTA. It's a beauty-spot. Sunday trippers stop to use the telescope. We went there often, he and I, as children. There's a river-bed below. We used to stand on the edge when bobba wasn't looking. Trying to make our stomachs churn. He knew it well. He'd seen it a hundred times. So why go back?

PAULA. Why not? A favourite place, why not go back? He didn't feel like climbing. That's why the shoes were wrong. No book. Was he a student?

MRS. KLEIN. He was a chemist in a paper-mill.

MELITTA. Hans went nowhere on his own without a book. That's what he was like. Except when he was fourteen, when you stopped him.

MRS. KLEIN. Stopped my son from reading books, darling that would be unique in Central Europe.

MELITTA. Mother you did.

MRS. KLEIN. I don't recall it and I don't believe it.

MELITTA. You told him the books were symptomatic of his hero-worship for his father. So he stopped.

MRS. KLEIN. He stopped himself.

MELITTA. You stopped his music lessons.

MRS. KLEIN. I did not, he stopped attending them. I went on paying for weeks since nobody told me.

MELITTA. He stopped because you told him that wanting to play the violin was a repressed masturbation fantasy.

MRS. KLEIN. It sounds extreme because you've isolated it.

MELITTA. You even stopped him being in love.

MRS. KLEIN. This is cheap.

MELITTA. He loved a boy at school. You broke them up.

MRS. KLEIN. If Hans were truly homosexual I'd have accepted it.

Although I might not like it. But he isn't, wasn't. And that boy was miles beneath him.

MELITTA. Then that actress, and you said she was a mother-figure with a penis.

MRS. KLEIN. Did you see her?

MELITTA. Then that very decent Polish girl. You stopped that too, you said she interfered with the analysis.

MRS. KLEIN. She did. That summer we were getting nowhere, then her father was transferred, she left town and we made good progress.

PAULA. Who was 'we'?

MRS. KLEIN (*to* MELITTA). So, tell her.

MELITTA. My mother analysed Hans for three hundred and seventy hours from the time he was thirteen to the age of sixteen and a half. She analysed us both. We were her first patients. She wrote us up. I'm Lisa in 'The Role of School in Libidinal Development'. Remember? How does it go? 'She has so far (she is now fifteen) shown only an average intelligence'. That was me. That's what's she wrote about me.

MRS. KLEIN (*to* PAULA). It seemed important to remain detached.

MELITTA. But mother.

Pause.

MRS. KLEIN. Yes I know.

PAULA. She was your daughter.

MRS. KLEIN. Yes.

Pause.

MELITTA. I'd lie there trying to think up what to say to her. Trying to think of something so banal, so ordinary that she couldn't interpret it. My history lesson. 'What's history about?' she'd ask me. In her clinical voice. My mother in her clinical voice, imagine. I'd say: 'Oh, history lessons, that's what people did in ancient times, battles and so on.' She'd say: 'What happened in ancient times is you, the infant, seeing your father and me having sexual intercourse. *That's* the battle.' It sounds absurd. It wasn't. That was the worst of it: she's so damn good. I felt that slotting into place, the snap, the 'Yes, that's right'. And I'd be stuck with a horrible

truth about myself I couldn't deal with. I wanted to protect her
from it, but she wouldn't let me. Kept on sucking it out. My poison.
Kept returning it. She used to light her cigarette, her special way,
the match pushed forward so the sparks shot into my lap. That was
my hatred flying back. The carved brown cabinet stood there
waiting my command to fall and crush her. Or the mat to trip her
up. She spilled the ashtray. Muck on the varnished floor. My
vengeful shit. All that was good, destroyed. My mother destroyed.
My fault. My guilt.

MRS. KLEIN. I did good work.

MELITTA. And the results?

MRS. KLEIN. You're not so bad. It's Dr. Schmideberg I'm not too
fond of.

MELITTA. I'm Dr. Schmideberg. Can't you understand?

MRS. KLEIN. I'm Melanie Klein.

Pause.

Is there more about Hans?

MELITTA. Yes. Somebody saw him.

MRS. KLEIN. When he – ?

MELITTA. No. Before. The Lutheran pastor in Ruzomberok. Jolan
told me. They're old friends. She trusts him.

MRS. KLEIN. Well?

MELITTA. He was waiting for a train first thing that morning. He was
on the platform at the station. And he noticed Hans.

MRS. KLEIN. The railway station?

MELITTA. Yes. The pastor asked him where he was going. Hans said,
to Budapest. The pastor said, good, we'll travel together. Hans said
no. He said he wanted to smoke. He seemed nervous. The pastor
said, is something wrong? Hans said no. The pastor didn't believe
him.

MRS. KLEIN. Why was Hans going to Budapest?

MELITTA. To see Aunt Jolan. So he said.

MRS. KLEIN. Go on.

MELITTA. He asked the pastor to forgive him.

MRS. KLEIN. Is there more?

MELITTA. He hoped the pastor wouldn't be shocked by something he might hear about him. He said he was sure that what he was doing was right.

MRS. KLEIN. That's all?

MELITTA. That's all.

MRS. KLEIN. So he planned to go to Jolan perhaps to find some comfort in her.

MELITTA. But he changed his mind. He never caught the train.

MRS. KLEIN. He went to the square and caught the bus. Yes, that feels right. I see it.

Pause.

Will it affect the place of burial?

MELITTA. No.

MRS. KLEIN. Because they – ?

MELITTA. Nobody knows what happened.

MRS. KLEIN. Just us. That's good.

About to pour herself another glass. To MELITTA.

You'll have some now?

Pours a glass. MELITTA *accepts it.*

MRS. KLEIN. What none of us cares to ask is why a healthy, reasonably happy man of twenty-seven should – . Paula, you're too polite to ask. (*To* MELITTA:) You're too defensive. I'm too frightened. No I'm damn well not.

PAULA. None of us knows he – .

MRS. KLEIN. We know.

PAULA. He didn't leave a message.

MRS. KLEIN. He did. Though it was probably unconscious. It was meant for me. He chose a place which looks across the valley towards Ruzomberok. Rosenberg. Rose mountain. The breast. Now that's indicative.

PAULA. It isn't your fault.

MRS. KLEIN. Don't reassure me.

PAULA. He could have been in trouble. He could have been ill.

MRS. KLEIN. A man who's ill can live in hope. Or die in peace like normal people. If you're in trouble you can leave the country, you can go to prison. There are hundreds of alternatives. Which you choose is up to the inner unconscious make-up of the individual. And that lies deep. It's formed in infancy. When Hans was an infant, what was the first pre-occupation of his ego?

PAULA. The breast.

MRS. KLEIN. The breast. The breast on to which the child projects the warmth and goodness which he feels. The good breast.

And its opposite. When the child is angry, envious. When the child's anticipation turns from love for the good-but-yet-to-come, to hate for the good which seems so miserly with its goodness. This is the breast the infant, in its primitive mind, attacks. Tramples, kicks, annihilates. Pinches, mangles, gnaws, tears apart. Devours. Pierces. Poisons with imagined faeces. And in short, destroys by all the means which infant sadism can devise. This is the breast on to which the child projects – *projects* – his murderous hatred. So that the breast itself seems hateful. Vengeful. Mercilessly cruel. The bad breast. And the prototype for adult fear and dread.

You'll have some more?

Pours wine.

No wish to boss you about my dear, but you'll be very little help to your neurotic patients till you lead them by the hand back to that primitive jungle. Which is wild and strange as only a jungle can be. And *illimitably* rich. You can do it. You've had a child. (*Of* MELITTA:) She has problems in this area, no, she knows my feelings, I can say this.

MELITTA, *unnoticed by her mother, starts to cry.*

It's when the infant *recognises* you that something new occurs. He starts the greatest struggle in human life. He sees his mother as a person. Whole, complete. Good and bad together. She, whom he's been torturing in his mind, is the one he loves. This is the dawn of guilt. It leads to fathomless depression. It is out of that depression he must climb in order to become a healthy adult. And it's hard. It hurts. To see what we've done to the one we love, it hurts, it hurts. (*To* MELITTA:) Don't drink.

She removes something from MELITTA*'s glass with the tip of her finger.*

Piece of cork. It's gone. Now you're in tears. You wanted to hurt the wicked mother. Now you find she's also the good and loving mother. Hurt the one, you hurt them both, darling I am one and the same. You cry. That's good. If I could cry like that I'd be a happy woman.

MELITTA. It isn't true. There are bad mothers. Mothers who are totally bad. You're one. We never felt you loved us. You were interested in us, that's all. But we loved you. He loved you terribly, terribly. And you could never accept his love for what it was. You always changed it. Made it yours. Everything had to be yours. Whatever we did, whatever we had, whatever we wanted. You'd make us think it wasn't really happening, or we didn't like it. Or you'd choose it for us. Anything. A dress in a shop, a train-set, my degree.

MRS. KLEIN. I chose your husband?

MELITTA. I was compensating.

MRS. KLEIN. Quite.

MELITTA. I was neurotically dependent on you.

MRS. KLEIN. So you made a break for freedom.

MELITTA. Yes I bloody well did.

MRS. KLEIN. What's interesting is that you chose a man my age. A mother-substitute. And what a disaster he turned out to be. A drunk, a fool. You fled from bondage into bondage. And you always will as long as you are crippled by your unresolved ambivalence towards me. So, resolve it. I can't. Nobody can but you. It's your job. Do it.

Pause.

The alternative is suicide. Either actual, as in Hans's case. Or else, symbolic, which is how you're going at present. And I can't lose any more children. Help me, darling. Forget the Institute. Forget the rows, the meetings. That's for weekdays. Tonight you are in my house. We're mother and daughter. And I'm saying, Melitta, Melchen, dearest, sweetheart, what must we do to have a sensible, adult, mother-and-daughter friendship?

MELITTA. You don't want one.

MRS. KLEIN. How am I stopping it? What do you want? Or don't you trust me?

MELITTA. No.

MRS. KLEIN. Good, so now there's something solid we can start with. Set me a challenge. Try me.

MELITTA. I can't think what to say.

MRS. KLEIN. No rush. Make yourself comfortable, free-associate.

MELITTA *sits up straight.*

So do it your own way.

MELITTA. I'm driving down to Glyndebourne next week.

MRS. KLEIN. I'm listening.

MELITTA. It's 'Cosi'. I got the last two tickets. I was planning to go with Walter. Now you're back I still intend to go with Walter.

MRS. KLEIN. Good, he should enjoy it.

MELITTA. There are six teaspoons in the kitchen drawer, they used to –

MRS. KLEIN. Take them. Paula dear, this must be dull for you, I'm sorry.

MELITTA. I've bought a dinner-service. I chose it myself. It's Lucy Cooper, polka-dots, I know you'll hate it.

MRS. KLEIN. This is superficial. When did either of us have our emotional homes in crockery departments. You're resisting something. Tell me.

MELITTA. There's a blanket in the boot of the car. It's mine. I want it.

MRS. KLEIN. You say the blanket but it's not the blanket.

MELITTA. I want the car. I want Sunny.

MRS. KLEIN. You *have* Sunny.

MELITTA. I have half of Sunny.

MRS. KLEIN. But you only paid for half.

MELITTA. I'll buy you out.

MRS. KLEIN. Though as things stand you have the use of Sunny whenever you ask.

MELITTA. I don't like asking.

MRS. KLEIN. So you want him to yourself.

MELITTA. That's right.

MRS. KLEIN (*thoughtful*). You think I can't be trusted not to damage the father's penis?

MELITTA. Mother, I do promise you, it isn't a penis. It's a 1927 Sunbeam. You say you let me use it. And you nearly always do. But when you can't, I feel irrationally resentful. And I think it would remove a source of tension between us if we did what adults mostly do, have cars of our own.

MRS. KLEIN. Good, fine.

MELITTA. I'll write you a cheque.

MRS. KLEIN. Not now, not now –.

MELITTA *writes a cheque.*

Well, as it suits you.

MELITTA *gives her the cheque.*

MELITTA. Two hundred and forty-seven pounds ten shillings. That's half the cost less depreciation plus the licence.

MRS. KLEIN. Thank you.

MELITTA. As you see, I plan to stay in London.

MRS. KLEIN. That will be nice for me.

MELITTA. So you can stop persuading your eminent friends to button-hole me at the Institute and tell me how much easier I might find it if I practised in New York.

MRS. KLEIN. They don't need my persuasion. People worry about you. New York is beautiful, the people are kind, demand is high, the fees are monstrous. I know the money-racket doesn't interest you but think of Walter. So we hoped you would consider it. Which you have. You choose to stay in London. As your mother I'm delighted. As your colleague I must warn you, I shall give no quarter. If your activities are inconsistent with your membership of the Society, I shall say so, so will others, you'll be forced to resign. You'll have to become some kind of therapist nonsense, thumping cushions with your patients. This may sound harsh, but it's the truth. Let's have things open and honest between us. As I know you want.

MELITTA. There's something else.

MRS. KLEIN. What?

MELITTA. I've changed my analyst.

Pause.

I said I –

MRS. KLEIN. I heard you.

Pause.

MRS. KLEIN. Just as you were getting somewhere. May I say, I think you're making a big mistake?

MELITTA. It's fine so far.

MRS. KLEIN. So far? So when did you start?

MELITTA. Three weeks ago.

MRS. KLEIN. I see. Of course I'm disappointed that you never thought to share your problem with me.

MELITTA. I discussed it with my analyst and decided not to.

MRS. KLEIN. You've rehearsed this conversation.

MELITTA. Yes.

MRS. KLEIN. I – . Yes quite right. Although it puts me in a strange position.

MELITTA. Me too.

MRS. KLEIN. What do I say to get her to take you back?

MELITTA *laughs.*

Is something funny?

MELITTA. Mother, I'm not going back.

MRS. KLEIN. Why not? You've made your gesture.

MELITTA. No.

MRS. KLEIN. You're adamant.

MELITTA. Yes.

MRS. KLEIN. And who've you gone to?

MELITTA. Edward Glover.

MRS. KLEIN *throws her wine at her.*

MRS. KLEIN. Drink that.

She grabs scraps of MELITTA*'s letter out of the waste paper basket.*

Eat these. Eat these. I'll stuff them down your throat. Poisoner. Eat. Eat.

She hits and attacks MELITTA, *rubbing bits of paper into her face and hair.* MELITTA *doesn't resist.* PAULA *pulls her off.* MRS. KLEIN *sits, surprised by her actions.* MELITTA *sits.* PAULA *watches. Each of them ends up in a different part of the room from before.*

PAULA (*to* MELITTA): Melitta?

MELITTA. Leave me alone, the pair of you.

MRS. KLEIN. Why don't we all sit quietly for a moment. Just we three.

Pause

I say we three. Though as a matter of fact we've quite a crowd collecting. (*To* MELITTA:) If you end up staying with Glover – . Which I don't advise. But if you do – .

MELITTA. Mother.

MRS. KLEIN. Listen. If you do. You'll need to watch the counter-transference. Remember his backward daughter. Glover sees you as the brilliant child he's always wanted.

MELITTA. I'd thought of that.

MRS. KLEIN. Of course, of course.

Pause.

And you should ask yourself who he is.

MELITTA. Glover?

MRS. KLEIN. Yes, to you. Just think about it.

MELITTA. I can tell you now. It's been a good three weeks. I see him as the father you betrayed.

MRS. KLEIN. That's your perspective. Now I'll tell you why he hates my work. He sees me as the wanton mother casting aside the wonderful father Freud.

MELITTA. He could be right.

PAULA. Melitta is my dead sister.

MRS. KLEIN. Well we all knew that. She's also you: the unloved daughter.

MELITTA. Rubbish.

MRS. KLEIN. That speaks volumes.

PAULA (*to* MRS. KLEIN). Who was she, when you were trying to drown her in symbolic urine?

MRS. KLEIN (*with irony*). Well I can't imagine.

MELITTA. When she rubbed symbolic faeces in my hair. (*With irony.*) Yes that's a tough one.

MRS. KLEIN. Really, Paula.

Pause.

MRS. KLEIN (*to* MELITTA). Though as a matter of fact I loved your bobba. I don't know why I got so nasty about her. All she was, was a typical bossy Central European Jewish mother. There are worse things. I hope. I see I can't amuse you.

MELITTA. Who was Hans?

MRS. KLEIN. My dream suggests as follows: that my envious triumph when my brother failed in something, just for once, was carried over into my feelings towards my son. I loved my son, but felt ambivalent towards him.

MELITTA. And you wished to harm him.

MRS. KLEIN. Wished it on some primitive level.

MELITTA. Primitive but effective.

MRS. KLEIN. So you think I killed him.

MELITTA. He killed you. He killed the you in him.

MRS. KLEIN. And why?

MELITTA. To punish it.

MRS. KLEIN. No this I can't go along with. He wished to save the me he loved from his sadistic onslaughts. So he killed them. And in doing so, killed himself. Now don't look blank, Melitta. Just because you never tried it. When did you save me from your sadistic onslaughts?

MELITTA. Mother, that's why I'm here. Hans died because he couldn't bring himself to hate you.

MRS. KLEIN. What about you, you can?

MELITTA. I can. I do.

MRS. KLEIN. Although there must be some ambivalence.

MELITTA. No. Not now.

MRS. KLEIN. You're saying you hate me pure and simple. Speak: I'm curious.

MELITTA. Yes.

MRS. KLEIN. Although we – sit and talk.

MELITTA. Never again.

She takes her key-ring out of her bag. Disentangles a single key.

MRS. KLEIN. No don't do that.

MELITTA (*holds them out*). My key.

MRS. KLEIN *looks at her cases.*

MRS. KLEIN. I shan't unpack tonight. Paula dear, you'll find a tiny bottle somewhere.

PAULA *looks in a case.*

And I'll need my nightdress.

MELITTA. I hung your blue one over the heater.

MRS. KLEIN. That was kind.

MELITTA. That's all it was.

MRS. KLEIN. I know.

Pause.

(*To* PAULA:) She was late, you know. Then finally I felt her pushing. In I went. And nothing. Nothing. Off you get, they said, we want the table. No, I cried, he's – . He. She was my first-born. I said, I feel him coming. But they heaved me off and I went waddling towards the door. And out she dropped. Just dropped. While I was standing up. And how they laughed. They said – in a nice way – that's how cows have babies. You should call your baby Buttercup. I said: I'll call her little Melanie. Melitta.

She looks at her watch.

Half-past-six.

PAULA *gives her the little bottle.*

MRS KLEIN. Thank you. My knockout drops.

PAULA *has also taken out an alarm-clock.*

MRS. KLEIN. Leave the alarm. I'll sleep in in the morning. Please don't wake me.

PAULA is about to help her with her coat.

MRS. KLEIN. I can manage.

She goes out.

PAULA. How do you feel?

MELITTA. The same. I'd love a slotting-into place, or snap or something. Get some sleep. I'll dress and go. Ssh!

PAULA. What?

MELITTA. She hasn't closed her door yet.

They listen. They hear a very slight noise.

PAULA. There.

MELITTA. No that's the bathroom.

They listen.

When will you start? With her, I mean.

PAULA. She hasn't agreed.

MELITTA. She will.

PAULA. I need her.

MELITTA. Yes.

PAULA. I need her in all kinds of ways.

MELITTA. I know. I always knew it. In my cynical soul. I knew it the moment I saw you working at that desk. I knew.

She holds up a hand to stop PAULA *replying. Listens, then goes out and upstairs.*

PAULA *finds the telephone number* MRS. KLEIN *gave her before leaving. Picks up the telephone, dials the operator.*

PAULA. Hello. I want – . I'm sorry, I can't speak any louder. I want to make a call to Budapest. 92435. No, personal. Mrs. Jolan Vago. V.A.– . Yes, I'll wait.

Rings off. Picks up a book. MELITTA *comes in, dressed.*

MELITTA. You're up.

PAULA. You left your doorkey.

MELITTA. I gave it back.

PAULA. She left it here.

MELITTA. She always does. I always take it. But it's different now.

Pause.

Except I always say it's different now. I tell you what. I'll wait till morning. And I'll see how it feels without.

PAULA. Without the key?

MELITTA. Without my mother. If it's fine, or not too bad or can be done without recourse to razors in the bath I'll – .

PAULA. What?

MELITTA. I'll write a book. And leave my husband. Have a child and go to China. In that order. But if not: I'll grovel down from Hampstead Garden Suburb in the morning at about eleven.

PAULA. Take the key.

MELITTA. I have my pride. I think I have my pride.

She picks the key up, then puts it down.

I have my pride. You do keep looking at the phone.

PAULA. I don't. Good night.

MELITTA. Good night.

MELITTA *goes out*. PAULA *starts making up her bed. The telephone rings. She answers quickly.*

PAULA. Mrs. Vago? ( ) Hello. I hope I haven't – . ( ) I'm calling from London, I'm a friend of Mrs. Klein's, I'm – . ( ) No I know she's not. She asked me to ring and tell you that she's very sorry but she won't be coming. ( ) Physically well but – . ( ) Yes she's very distressed. ( ) I will, Mrs. Vago, there was something I wanted to – . ( ) Yes, a family friend. ( ) Berlin. ( ) It is, yes, Mrs. Vago, there's a very important question I must ask you. It's about Hans. ( ) I know she did, I – . ( ) I think you know. I think there's something which you haven't told us. And I think you ought to. ( ) She's upset already.

The alarm-clock goes off. PAULA *tries to turn it off while still continuing the conversation. Can't find the switch.*

( ) No it's different here. ( ) It's just an alarm-clock, go on. ( ) I knew it. ( ) Yes. ( ) I see, and tell me about the wallet. ( ) And?

She turns the alarm-clock off.

She, won't she'll be relieved. You see, she thought he'd – . No, it doesn't matter. ( ) Very expensive, yes. ( ) I'm sure she will, perhaps later today, she's sleeping now. ( ) Likewise. ( ) God bless you too. Good-bye.

She rings off. Sits and thinks for a moment or two. Turns off the lights. She lies down on the sofa, covers herself with blankets, still thoughtful. Closes her eyes.

Music.

Time passes.

It is some hours later.

Cracks of daylight through the curtains.

PAULA is still asleep.

MRS. KLEIN comes in. She wears a a new dress. She goes quietly and without turning lights on to the filing-cabinet.

PAULA wakes.

PAULA. What time is it?

MRS. KLEIN. It's not eleven o'clock yet. Go back to sleep.

She rummages in the filing cabinet.

PAULA. I can't.

MRS. KLEIN. So: maybe it won't disturb you if I draw the curtains.

PAULA shakes her head. MRS. KLEIN draws the curtains. Bright spring day outside.

MRS. KLEIN. In my garden I have pigeons, blackbirds, finches, swifts and robins. And I sometimes hear an owl. I find this very reassuring for a London garden. Now you'll have some coffee?

PAULA. Thank you.

MRS. KLEIN. Don't get up.

MRS. KLEIN goes out. PAULA lights a cigarette. MRS. KLEIN comes back in with coffee. Gives it to PAULA, goes back to her files.

MRS. KLEIN. I'm hunting out my criminality paper. Since I fear it's in the firing-line. Now where've you got to, naughty fellow. Here.

Finds it.

There's something you could do. If you could stay till supper. Six o'clock. It's Hans's service then. We'll say a prayer in Hebrew. You remember any Hebrew?

PAULA. No.

MRS. KLEIN. Likewise. Too bad, we'll drink a glass of sherry maybe. What I must do before is make a difficult call to Jolan to explain my absence.

PAULA. I've told her.

MRS. KLEIN. What?

PAULA. I rang her up last night. I didn't wake you?

MRS. KLEIN. No you didn't but I'm wondering why you took it on yourself to trouble her?

PAULA. I did it for you. For you and Hans. I had to. Something didn't feel right. That letter about his Cossack costume. I recognised it. I've a mother and I write to her every week. She wants two pages or she'll think there's something wrong. And so she gets them. But I can't exactly tell her the truth about my life. It's too –.

MRS. KLEIN. Too what?

PAULA. It's mine. And so I fill it up with trivia. Just like he did. He was hiding something. So I moved the material round and found a different interpretation. And I felt that snap, that 'yes'. And rang Mrs. Vago.

MRS. KLEIN. So, I'm listening.

PAULA. Hans had fallen in love.

MRS. KLEIN. In love?

PAULA. The woman's older –. Older than he was.

MRS. KLEIN. How much older?

PAULA. In her thirties. She's a singer. Jolan likes her. She lives in Budapest. She has a husband there and children. Two: a boy and a girl.

MRS. KLEIN. Surprise me. And?

PAULA. I understood it all. It's simple. Hans was meeting her at the station. They planned to spend the Easter holiday together. He was waiting on the platform and he saw the pastor. He felt nervous.

So he lied: he said that he was going to Budapest, to see Aunt
Jolan, knowing the pastor knew her. He warned him there'd be
gossip. He asked him to forgive him. But he wasn't ashamed: he
knew that what he was doing was right. The train came in. They
took the bus. She put the tickets in her handbag. He didn't bring a
book or climbing boots. Why should he? They breakfasted
together and he left an enormous tip; he wanted to impress her.

MRS. KLEIN. Why the mountains?

PAULA. They'd booked a room in the tourist hotel. He left his
money there. She took it to Budapest and gave it back to Mrs.
Vago. She said he'd gone for a walk. While she was getting dressed.
Mid-afternoon. She waited. Then she went to find him, and she – .
That was the first she knew. It seems he'd tried to find a path that
isn't there now. And the ground had fallen away. That's all. That's
all.

Pause.

MRS. KLEIN. What's interesting is that I feel intense resentment.
Not of you, so much, you meant well. But this *woman*, who the hell
was she, what's her name?

PAULA. I don't know.

MRS. KLEIN. A singer?

PAULA. Yes.

MRS. KLEIN. Opera? Cabaret?

PAULA. Mrs. Vago didn't tell me.

MRS. KLEIN. Had they – ? Yes, that afternoon you say.

Pause.

I cannot adjust to this. I can't accept it. (*Angry.*) What the hell are
you trying to tell me, that he died by chance?

Pause. PAULA shocked and upset.

MRS. KLEIN. He never mentioned her. Not once, not once. Who are
her parents?

PAULA. I didn't ask. Where she comes from, where they met. It's
nothing to do with – .

Suddenly angry, shouts.

Don't you see? It's nothing to do with you, you stupid bloody
woman. He was free.

MRS. KLEIN. No no. The facts remain the same – .

Pause. She crumples.

Oh God, I've lost him.

She starts to cry. Cries for a long time. After a bit she holds her hand out.

Come.

PAULA *holds her hand. After a bit* MRS. KLEIN *stops crying.*

MRS. KLEIN. Real tears. So my denial is *greatly* weakened. Yes, I'm starting to recover.

Pause.

I said the facts remained the same. Well, *certain* facts. My guilt remains. So does my wish to make amends. Now my appointment book is somewhere.

She finds it. Opens it.

MRS. KLEIN. This is what you want?

PAULA. It is

MRS. KLEIN. Because you must be sure.

PAULA. I'm sure.

MRS. KLEIN *looks through her appointment-book.*

MRS. KLEIN. Where are we.

Looks upwards.

And the ceiling's moving upwards. I feel open. Easier. Tears, you know, are very much equated with excreta in the unconscious mind. Through tears the mourner eases tension, casts bad objects into the outside world. You know my fees?

PAULA. I do.

MRS. KLEIN. They're what's expected. You must decide to place that value on my time. And yours.

PAULA. I'll manage.

MRS. KLEIN. I can offer you Mondays, Wednesdays, Fridays, Saturdays. At eleven a.m. Now must I put these in my book, you tell me.

PAULA. Eleven o'clock is fine.

MRS. KLEIN *writes times in her book.*

PAULA. In fact we're late.

MRS. KLEIN. I beg your pardon?

PAULA. It's Saturday now. And look at the clock. We've lost five minutes.

MRS. KLEIN. My consulting-room is locked. And there's the stairs.

PAULA. Let's stay down here.

MRS. KLEIN. It's all too much, I'm utterly exhausted, not this morning. No.

PAULA. Please, Mrs. Klein.

MRS. KLEIN. I see. Very well. But from Monday we must be more formal.

PAULA lies on the sofa, pulls a blanket over her feet. MRS. KLEIN moves a chair into position.

MRS. KLEIN. And not the coffee please.

She removes the cup.

Pause. MRS. KLEIN sits.

MRS. KLEIN. Whenever you want.

She waits with a singular expression of alertness: her professional manner. Different from the way she's looked at any previous point in the play.

Pause.

PAULA. I'm worried about the doorbell.

MRS. KLEIN. You worry that if it rings I might abandon you.

PAULA. I know you won't. You told me yesterday. You said the world must wait.

Pause.

I know this isn't helpful, but I can't help thinking as an analyst. You feel guilty about your children.

MRS. KLEIN. Mm hm.

PAULA. You see the harm you've done.

MRS. KLEIN. Go on.

PAULA. You want to pay them reparation. But for one of them it's too late.

MRS. KLEIN. Mm hm.

PAULA. You want to pay Melitta reparation.

Pause.

You're doing so now.

Pause.

I terribly want you to reply to that.

MRS. KLEIN. You were afraid I'd left you.

PAULA. No. I felt content.

MRS. KLEIN. You felt – .

The doorbell rings. MRS. KLEIN *does not react to it.*

MRS. KLEIN. You feel perhaps that you've replaced Melitta as my daughter.

Doorbell.

PAULA. I have.

Doorbell.

MRS. KLEIN. Mm hm.

PAULA. I feel – .

MRS. KLEIN. I'm listening.

Doorbell.

End of Play